Original title:
The Orchid's Elegy

Copyright © 2025 Creative Arts Management OÜ
All rights reserved.

Author: Atticus Thornton
ISBN HARDBACK: 978-1-80581-922-6
ISBN PAPERBACK: 978-1-80581-449-8
ISBN EBOOK: 978-1-80581-922-6

Shadows in the Blossoming Glade

In the glade where shadows dance,
Giggling plants take their chance.
Bumblebees waltz, thinking they're slick,
While flowers joke, 'Here comes the tick!'

Curtains of petals sway and tease,
They whisper secrets to the bees.
Yet one shy bud blushes in lieu,
Saying, 'Why am I not funny too?'

Reflections on Nature's Grace

In the pond, the lilies float,
One took a ride on a small goat.
With every ripple, a laugh appears,
Echoes of laughter drown out fears.

Swaying trees crack jokes so clear,
Telling tales of the sneaky deer.
As clouds drift in with a cheeky grin,
Nature's comedy show will begin!

Lament of the Lonely Stem

A lonely stem stands all alone,
Complaining softly in a tone.
'Why did they pick all my friends?'
'Who knew plants had such trends?'

Swaying weeds pass with a snicker,
Saying, 'Cheer up, your bloom's a sticker!'
But still, he sighs with wilted flair,
Dreaming of blooms that never were there.

The Art of Letting Go

Petals drift like a playful sigh,
A flower's farewell, oh me, oh my!
Each wrinkled leaf whispers a joke,
'I'm free now, like a feathered cloak.'</br>

With a twirl, they dance in the breeze,
While roots below giggle with ease.
Letting go is certainly fun,
Better than being stuck in the sun!

Glistening Dewdrops of Sorrow

Dewdrops dance on leaves, a show,
They slip and slide, oh what a flow!
Flowers giggle, swaying with cheer,
While bees are stuck, oh dear, oh dear.

Pollen party, come join the spree,
But watch your step, a dance with a bee!
Nature's pranks, so wild and bright,
In each dewdrop, laughter takes flight.

The Grief of Lush Enchantment

In fields so green, the grass does moan,
'Tis not the roses, but weeds overgrown.
A snail slips by in splendid frown,
While daisies chuckle, wearing their crown.

Sunflower waves, but oh, what's this?
It turned too much; now it's a miss!
The sun's too bright, they shout with glee,
Yet now they hide, just wait and see.

Wistful Colors of Farewell

Petals blush in shades of despair,
As colors clash in the evening air.
But flowers laugh, 'It's just a trend!'
They wink at buds, 'We'll only pretend!'

Autumn whispers, 'Time to depart!'
Yet daisies rally, with courage and heart.
They throw a party, petals all around,
And when they leave, it's joy that's found.

A Tapestry of Fallen Fragrance

The scent of blooms wafts through the breeze,
But flies decide it's time to tease!
They buzz about in fragrant dreams,
While flowers roll their eyes and schemes.

Under the moon, a fragrance fight,
Roses insist, their time's just right.
But dandelions laugh with glee,
'We bloom with chaos, just wait and see!'

Traces of Blossom's Mourning

In a pot, she lost her grace,
Now dust bunnies take her space.
She used to sway, now she droops,
Her petals, once grand, are now loops.

Photos of her glory days,
I wish I had some better sprays.
But water went to just a trickle,
Now she just looks sad and fickle.

Timelessness in Each Fallen Fragment

Each petal falls like yesterday,
A little laugh on life's ballet.
Her colors faded, what a scene,
Now even weeds are evergreen.

The gardener sighs with great despair,
He reads her eulogy with care.
But then he trips on fallen hues,
And laughs aloud, sticking with blues.

A Garden's Quiet Reflection

In silence, she laments her past,
Where blooms were bright, not shadows cast.
The butterflies all flew away,
Left her to ponder, 'What a day!'

A daisy joked, 'You're still the best!'
'Just wilted,' she said, 'don't be a pest.'
They chuckled soft, their friendship true,
In sadness, they found laughter anew.

The Heart of a Wilted Stem

A wilted stem with stories told,
Of summer's warmth and winter's cold.
She quipped, 'My glory's in the past,
But wait! Aren't weeds the ones who last?'

The sunlight teased her, barely warm,
She rolled her eyes, 'This isn't charm!'
Yet laughter sprouted, bold and bright,
Even in wilt, there's pure delight.

Whispers of Petal Shadows

In a garden where flowers giggle,
Petals dance, they shimmy and wiggle.
Bees buzz by, wearing tiny hats,
Chasing scents like cheeky acrobats.

Sunlight spills in a silly sunbeam,
Flowers blush, caught in a daydream.
Thorns pretend to be tough and gruff,
But soft petals say, 'Enough is enough!'

Elegance in Twilight

At dusk, the blossoms hold a ball,
Their flouncy gowns drape long and tall.
Crickets chirp in tuxedos fine,
While moonlight pours a glass of wine.

Petals gossip and share sweet tales,
Of butterflies riding on the gales.
But when the night gets far too late,
They trip on roots and laugh at fate.

Fragile Beauty's Lament

Oh, fragile blooms, such delicate sprites,
Whine about bugs in their designer tights.
They sigh for the rain, then hide from the glow,
The drama of life in a bloom's daily show.

They laugh at the daisies, all rough and green,
Claim their perfume is fit for a queen.
Yet in a breeze, their petals may fly,
'Catch me if you can!' the flowers cry.

Veil of Petals and Time

Underneath a veil of dainty grace,
Petals plot a most hilarious chase.
Time ticks slowly, but flowers are fast,
Chasing fleeting moments that never last.

With laughter and bloom, they push through the hours,
Turning sunshine into sweet-scented showers.
In the riot of colors, life's a great game,
As every petal shouts out its name.

The Garden's Quiet Grief

In the garden where blooms all sigh,
Petals flutter and silently cry.
A gnome lost in thought, a snail on a spree,
Both laugh in their own garden decree.

We water with tears, we prune with a frown,
While daisies gossip of the old and the brown.
Each weed tells a joke, a wisecrack or two,
While the roses just blush when the wind blows right through.

Lush Remnants of a Withering Heart

Once vibrant with laughter, now slightly dismayed,
A tulip in taffeta, feeling quite played.
Its petals now droopy, seeking a hug,
While the daisies just giggle: "Give it a shrug!"

The bees hold a meeting, they buzz and they jest,
About flowers who wilt and how they need rest.
A pansy pipes up, with a chuckle quite loud,
"It's all just a phase; let's dance in our shroud!"

Veil of Morning Dew

Morning dew drips like laughter from leaves,
As sunbeams join in, and chaos weaves.
Petunias get tipsy in light's golden glow,
Dancing on breezes, putting on a show.

A mockingbird sings of the day's little pranks,
While cucumbers giggle in the garden's flanks.
"Let's mingle with bees," a marigold teases,
"Where flowers are wild and humor never ceases!"

Beauty's Transient Whimsy

A daffodil whispers, "Oh, where have you been?"
To a tulip lost in a fantasy spin.
With laughter they twirl, in a vortex of blooms,
And chuckle at shadows that dance in the glooms.

As petals grow weary and colors start to fade,
A sunflower beams, saying, "Don't be afraid!"
For in gardens we jest and in moments we fade,
With laughter our memories, forever we've made!

A Hymn for Faded Beauty

In a garden of grace, once so bold,
The flowers now giggle, their petals old.
They whisper sweet secrets of times that were,
To blooms full of life, oh what a blur!

With wrinkled faces, they drink their tea,
Recalling adventures, how wild they could be.
Yet now they're all pruned, just a tad less spry,
Making jokes 'bout their age, oh me, oh my!

The stems may be bent, but spirits stay bright,
They joke with the daisies, through day and the night.
For beauty may fade, like an old, worn shoe,
But laughter and joy can still bloom anew.

So here's to the blooms, with a wink and a sway,
Reminding us all to laugh come what may.
Though the colors are dim, their humor's in play,
In this garden of jest, where the old flowers stay.

Petals on the Water

Petals afloat on the water so wide,
They're taking a cruise, on a lazy tide.
They giggle and float, what a silly sight,
Dressed in their hues, oh so bright in the light!

They wave at the fish with an elegant flair,
"Join us!" they cry, "Come float without care!"
But the fish just laugh, as they swim and they dive,
"Petals can't swim; we know you'll arrive!"

Drifting and laughing, the petals compete,
For best of the day, oh what a treat!
With each little splash, they tumble and roll,
In this watery dance, they've found their true soul.

Though their time is short, they splash without fear,
In a world full of joy, it's the fun we hold dear.
For with every ripple, there's laughter and cheer,
Petals on the water, let's raise a cold beer!

Transformation of Diminished Grace

Oh, once I stood tall, with grace and with pride,
Now I'm leaning and giggling, what a bumpy ride!
Each bloom that once sparkled, a faded old mess,
But laughter is timeless, I must confess!

In the mirror of petals, I see my old face,
Just cracked in a way that's a funny embrace.
With my leaves all a-flutter, I dance in the breeze,
Like an old grandpa trying to catch the bees!

Stumbling through gardens, I trip with great flair,
Every tumble's a story that's light as the air.
For time is a prankster, but oh what a jest,
As I laugh off my wrinkles, I feel truly blessed.

So here's to the future, with all of its quirks,
Embrace every wrinkle, enjoy all the perks.
For fading's just part of this grand masquerade,
With humor, my beauty will never quite fade!

Whispers of Yesterday's Blooms

In the shadows they giggle, those blooms of the past,
With whispers of jokes that were shared ever so fast.
"Oh remember that bee? What a blunder it made!
Buzzed right through a petal, in quite a parade!"

Each sunset recalls little tales from the light,
How the violets faded, gave daisies a fright.
"Remember that time?" they cackle and sway,
When the gardener tripped, sending weeds on the way!

Those echoes of laughter, so gentle and sweet,
Turn every dry bud into a comic feat.
For beauty may wither, but joys keep us spry,
And the whispers of blossoms will never say die.

With petals a-flutter, they dance through the air,
While sharing their stories without a care.
For each faded flower is still full of cheer,
In this garden of humor, where laughter draws near.

Blossom's Last Serenade

In the garden of giggles, blooms lost their flair,
Dancing in sunlight without a single care.
With petals that flutter, they made quite the show,
But whispered their secrets to the pesky crow.

A bee made a snicker, the wind caught a sigh,
If only these petals could just learn to fly!
Their colors were vibrant, yet fading away,
As visitors chuckled, 'Here's the end of play!'

Fragile Beauty's Lament

A delicate flower, with laughter in its veins,
Who knew such a joy came wrapped in disdain?
It joked with the buds while sipping on dew,
But sighs escape softly, like whispers anew.

Yet as sunlight dwindles, they tumble and sway,
Making the bees dance in a frolicsome fray.
With petals all wrinkled and a wink in its eye,
It giggles at life, 'Oh my, how we fly!'

In the Shade of Withering Blooms

Underneath the large trees where shadows now creep,
Blooms share a secret, oh promises they keep.
With a chuckle and blush, they wave to the breeze,
Sipping on sunlight, with more giggles than ease.

Yet time takes its toll, and the laughter grows dim,
As petals are spilling like water from brim.
In this shadowy corner where beauty once swayed,
The echoes of laughter still serenely parade.

Echoes of a Silent Blossom

A blossom once bright, now quiet and sly,
Whispers of humor pass by with a sigh.
It chuckles at shadows that come out at night,
While dreaming of bright days bathed in pure light.

With petals half drooping, it tells silly tales,
To crickets who listen and take little trails.
In the stillness of twilight, these echoes expand,
Creating a symphony all over the land.

Melancholy of the Whispering Leaves

Leaves chatted softly in the breeze,
Lamenting their lives with such unease.
A squirrel nearby laughed with delight,
Sipping acorn tea, oh what a sight!

Once vibrant green, now slightly pale,
They told their tales without much gale.
A bug flew by, wearing a hat,
"Why so gloomy? It's just habitat!"

With every gust, a giggle slipped,
As leaves on branches lightly quipped.
"Why worry 'bout a drop of rain?"
"When you can dance and feel no strain!"

They swayed and joked, though fate was bleak,
With every flutter, they found their peak.
"Who needs a garden? We're quite chic!
Just pass the bugs, I feel unique!"

Reverie of a Forgotten Flora

Once a flower of great renown,
Now a wilting, frowning brown.
Remembered in books, but not in sun,
Oh, the laughter! Oh, the fun!

Forgotten fossil of floral fame,
In violets days, it felt no shame.
But now it waits, a ghostly sight,
"Where'd everyone go? I miss the light!"

A fading petal, with dreams of flair,
"I'll throw a party, if only they care!"
Yet found no guests among the weeds,
Just spiders plotting, sharing their deeds.

So here it sits, imagining grand,
"Next spring, I'll rise, a bold flower band!"
With blooms and buds, a vibrant show,
I'll dance once more, just wait and know!

Petal-Draped Memories

Memories linger in shades of pink,
A petal parade, oh, just think!
Each bloom a giggle from days gone past,
A floral fiesta, fun unsurpassed!

"Oh dear sun, please don't be shy,
Can't you see we're meant to fly?"
With nectar smiles, they swayed in sync,
Worrying little about the drink.

In a pot so small, they wove a tale,
With dancing roots and a heavy veil.
"I spilled my water, a dreadful flop,
But do come dance, let's make it pop!"

They shared their thoughts on colorful dreams,
Of buzzing bees and moonlit beams.
Petal-draped laughs, all around they twirled,
As a fragrant gossip fairly swirled!

Shattered Bouquets and Midnight Hues

A bouquet tossed in the midnight air,
Landed so awkward, like a play with flair.
"Just a trip! How silly we seem,
Now we're scattered, not quite a team!"

Each stem whispered secrets of love,
Even the stars couldn't help but shove.
With giggles and gasps, they made a scene,
"Oh, let's not fret! We look like a dream!"

Broken shards of what used to be,
Yet laughter grew like wild, tall trees.
"I'll wear a petal, just call me chic,
Together we'll blossom, not so meek!"

So shattered bouquets danced through the night,
Midnight hues flashing with sheer delight.
In every crease, a spark did bloom,
Celebrating failure, flipping the gloom!

Memories of a Silken Stem

In a garden bright, where flowers sway,
A silly stem danced the day away.
With petals flapping, quite out of tune,
It thought it could jive with the lazy moon.

Bees buzzed by, with a quizzical frown,
Wondering why that stem wore a crown.
The more it wobbled, the more they all laughed,
As roots tangled in a comedic craft.

One day a breeze gave a flap and a twist,
The stem took a dive, as if it had missed.
With laughter echoing through the green,
It found joy in chaos, oh what a scene!

Now memories linger of that funny time,
When a silken stem thought it could rhyme.
Amidst fallen blooms, it still holds its pride,
In each petal's chuckle, its spirit won't hide.

The Solitude of Fallen Blooms

Once blooms so proud in the summer's glare,
Now lie in solitude, a comedic affair.
They poke fun at the vines draped on the wall,
'We're quite the catch, let's have a ball!'

With petals drooping and stems quite bare,
They argue over who has the best hair.
One claims it's the mold adding character flair,
While another insists it's the dirt that they share.

They reminisce of the days in the sun,
When they'd flaunt their beauty, oh what fun!
Now rolling in laughter, they share their old dreams,
And giggle at life's rather slippery seams.

In their quiet corner, the whimsies fly,
Bantering about each bloom that passed by.
With humor in petals, they've made their own place,
In this lonely garden, a laugh-filled space.

A Dance of Dying Colors

In hues so bright, they twirled and spun,
A party of colors, oh so much fun!
Each petal took flight, with a shimmy and shake,
Until they discovered their life was at stake.

With fading glories, they fell to the ground,
Discussing their losses, while laughing around.
'Have you seen my shade? It's gone off to hide!'
One giggled aloud, while another sighed.

An old leaf chimed in with a wise, crackling tone,
'Remember sweet blooms, you're never alone!
Even in dying, there's humor to find,
Just look at us now, though tattered, we shine.'

In a dance of dying, new tales they spun,
Finding joy in decay, each moment a pun.
A colorful uproar beneath the blue sky,
In the heart of the garden, laughter won't die.

Wistful Breezes and Pale Petals

In the whisper of winds, pale petals would sigh,
Sharing stories of bees and clouds drifting by.
'Oh, the days we've bloomed, how we danced with glee!'
They chuckled at tales of their former spree.

A breeze tickled soft, making petals take flight,
Spinning round like dancers in the warm light.
But alas, as the colors began to fade,
They giggled at how quickly they all went parades.

Wistfully they laughed at their upcoming end,
'Time to make room for the next trend!'
Though pale and weathered, they showed off their grace,
With humor inscribed on each lovely face.

As night descended and they swayed to sleep,
Their chuckles echoed, memories to keep.
Wistful breezes, they fatefully call,
In a garden of laughter, they'll always stand tall.

Twilight's Floral Farewell

In the garden where blooms once thrived,
A hilariously drooping flower survived.
It waved goodbye with a twist and a sway,
As all the bees fled in dismay.

Petals falling like confetti rife,
Celebrating the end of its flowery life.
With roots that went searching for humor anew,
It chuckled at weeds that were far from a view.

Sunset giggles danced on the breeze,
While the daisies just chuckled at their knees.
"Don't mind me," croaked the last stem of green,
"I was just practicing for the floral scene!"

As twilight closed in on the laughable plot,
The plants shared their jokes, and time forgot.
In this garden of laughter, nobody mourns,
For even the petals were laughing in thorns.

Dance of the Drooping Stems

Once stood a flower with quite the flair,
But now it's swaying with no one to care.
Its leaves gave up, and its petals took flight,
In a hilarious tango that lasted all night.

A squirrel rolled by, with a grin on its face,
Joined the stems in a jitterbug race.
"Oh, don't look now, I've tripped on your roots!"
Cried the hedgehog, while donning a pair of cute boots.

The moon watched on, it couldn't help but laugh,
As the stems twisted and turned on a gnarled path.
"Let's form a conga!" the sunflower said,
And they danced 'til the ground seemed to sway beneath their bed.

Under starlit giggles, their fun took its toll,
A garden party that somehow felt whole.
For in each droop lay a story unmatched,
Of laughter and joy, none ever detached.

A Shade of Elegance

In the corner, a violette spins in delight,
With a dainty bow tie that's quite a sight.
"Oh look at me, with such flair and poise!"
While neighboring daisies poke fun with their noise.

They laughed, "Oh dear, with such fancy clothes,
You might fly away with a gust that just grows!"
But elegance twirled, never losing its zest,
"Just watch as I outshine you all in this quest!"

With an air of fresh humor, it struck a pose,
While bumblebees buzzed, caught off-guard in their prose.

Each petal a laugh, a dance of pure glee,
As the violette pirouetted with glee.

At twilight, the garden glowed with the cheer,
Even weeds joined in, waving without any fear.
It's all just a jest, as they swayed in the sun,
For in nature's embrace, everyone's having fun.

Petals Adrift on Sorrow

A flower once blushed in a radiant hue,
But now it ponders, "What's this I must do?"
Petals drift towards a pond's deep regret,
Whispering secrets they can't quite forget.

"Why does my neighbor dance with such grace?
While I'm here sulking, just lost in my space?"
A lily raised its stem with a wink of its eye,
"Cheer up, dear friend; life's too short to cry!"

With each gentle breeze, the petals took flight,
Twisting and turning, they embraced the night.
"Join us," they cheered, "in this sorrowful game,
Life can be funny, though it might seem lame!"

So laughter ensued, in that garden forlorn,
As love for the dance became widely reborn.
Even in sadness, there's joy to be found,
As petals adrift shared laughter all around.

Coda of the Flourishing Heart

In the garden, blooms a mess,
Petals dance in their Sunday dress.
A bee winks and flies right by,
While I trip on roots and sigh.

Sun shines bright upon my knee,
Plants giggle as they see me flee.
Oh, the flowers think they know,
That I'm the star of this show!

Snails hold their party in the night,
As I seek out a safer flight.
Their slow groove is quite a sight,
It's hard not to laugh at their plight.

Yet, when rain falls, spirits lift,
The blooms and I share a gift.
We laugh and slip, we all agree,
Nature's jokes are wild and free.

Twilight Whispers Among Stems

At twilight's call, the shadows grow,
Plants chat freely, putting on a show.
A fern plays tag with the timid breeze,
While daisies chuckle at my unease.

A caterpillar's grand escape,
Turns to a dance, oh what a shape!
He's spinning tales beneath the moon,
I wish I could join, but I trip too soon.

Crickets chirp a merry tune,
While I consider a clumsy swoon.
The blooms all hum, "What's that sound?"
I blush to know they've gathered 'round.

Yet laughter sways with every sway,
Underneath the stars' ballet.
It's a funny garden brigade,
With secrets shared that never fade.

The Gentle Weeping of Blossoms

A flower's frown I catch today,
"Why'd you step on me?" it seemed to say.
I groaned and knelt, gave it a kiss,
"It wasn't me, it's just my bliss!"

Petals drop like silly crowns,
While I, the jester, fumble 'round.
The roses laugh, so bright and bold,
"Stop counting blooms, you look so old!"

With every tumble, laughter grows,
Their jokes are sweeter than the prose.
Yet when they sigh, I give a grin,
"Just wait, my friends, the fun begins!"

With tears of joy, they share their glee,
While I wipe dirt from my knee.
A weeping flower? A funny sight,
In this patch, we bloom with delight.

Lament at the Edge of the Garden

At garden's edge, I stop and sigh,
The flowers here, oh my, oh my!
With weeds that giggle and roots that trip,
I ponder if I'll get a grip.

"Cut the chatter!" a daisy shouts,
While the tulips dance, full of doubts.
I dance too, a sight to see,
But a tumble sends me to my knee.

"Come join us, clown!" the lilies cheer,
As mud suddenly becomes my sphere.
Splashing blooms and raucous laughter,
These garden antics bring delight thereafter.

So, here's to blooms that jest and play,
In this wild world, I long to stay.
With every step, I face my lot,
And find that laughter hits the spot.

Sorrow Bodied in Floral Glass

In a vase, a flower pouts,
With wilted petals full of doubts.
It hopes for sun, but gets a draft,
Where's the joy in this floral craft?

A bee buzzed by, said with a grin,
"Your fragrance? Oh, it's wearing thin!"
The flower sighed, "I need a spa,
A little light? I could use a paw!"

Friends who come by seldom stay,
They bring their chatter, then drift away.
The flower thinks it's quite a jest,
To bloom alone, it's not the best!

So here it sits, a frown so grim,
Awaiting the light on a hopeful whim.
But once in bloom, it'll be a blast,
"Take a whiff! This funk won't last!"

Beneath the Weeping Boughs

Under branches that shed tears,
Lies a plant with all its fears.
"Why so sad?" a squirrel did scoff,
"With all this shade, just shake it off!"

The flower sulked, its leaves askew,
"I'm feeling damp, and lost too!"
The squirrel chuckled, patted its head,
"You need some sun, not this sad bed!"

A drop of rain, a tiny splash,
Gave rise to blooms in a sudden flash.
The flower laughed, a quirky sound,
"I guess my woes just turn around!"

Then it twirled, feeling quite spry,
Even squirrels could not deny.
Beneath the boughs, there's joy in gloom,
Who knew it could dance and bloom?

Nature's Softest Farewell

In gentle wind, the petals sway,
"They'll miss me," the flower did say.
But a butterfly sat close by,
"What's a goodbye without a high?"

"You're not gone, just taking breath,
In every bloom, there's life, not death!"
The flower perked, its leaf did twirl,
"Maybe my fate is more of a whirl!"

With sunlight peeking, it felt quite bold,
"Farewell? Not me, I'm still gold!"
From dull despair to vibrant cheer,
Nature chuckled, this flower's near.

With each soft touch, and sway so grand,
The flower learned to understand.
It blooms anew, with pure delight,
A farewell party, what a sight!

Bouquet of Forgotten Whispers

In a garden where gossip thrives,
A group of flowers share their jives.
"Did you hear?" one giggled loud,
"That fern's convinced it's in a crowd!"

Petals flutter, secrets loom,
As bees join in with their own tune.
"We'll send a card, to say we care,
But ferns don't read, that's just unfair!"

A dandelion chimed in with glee,
"I've a secret, just between me!"
Rippling laughter danced on air,
With petals shaken in wild flair.

So here they sit, on stalks so tall,
Whispering sweet nothings to all.
A bouquet full of silly dreams,
In the garden's heart, life brightly beams!

A Poem for the Vanishing Bloom

A flower prances in the sun,
With petals bright and so much fun.
But lo! A squirrel, sly and quick,
Takes a nibble, oh what a trick!

It quivers, shakes, then starts to pout,
'Who's that thief? Get him out!'
The bloom debates, should it just fade?
Or dance around and join the parade?

The bees buzz too, in frantic flaps,
With buzzing laughter, shoulder taps.
In gardens lush, why worry so?
There's cake to share and seeds to sow!

With giggles and snorts, they stand so tall,
A party's coming, bloom or fall!
In petals bright, they find their cheer,
And toast to laughter, year by year!

Sorrow in the Garden

In a garden lush, a bloom felt blue,
Complaining of woes, and a dreadful view.
'I'm wilting fast, can't find a friend,
Is this the way that petals end?'

A gnome nearby, with a cheeky grin,
Said, 'YOU'RE too bright for a frown to win!
Just throw a party, let laughter spring,
Dance on the breeze, let joy take wing!'

The weeds all cheered, the ants did sway,
'Yay for the blooms! Let's party today!'
And in that garden, through giggle and glee,
The sorrow faded, just like a bee.

So, if you find a flower down,
Remember, it's okay to clown.
With jest and jive, not gloom and doom,
You'll always find joy in the sweetened bloom!

Reflections on a Wilted Past

Oh wilted leaf, so sad you lie,
But let's not dwell on the goodbye.
You once were bold, a sight to see,
Now you whisper to bumblebees!

A gardener walks with clumsy feet,
Tripping on roots, now that's a feat!
He trips for the bloom, and down he goes,
On top of you, it comically shows!

The sun still laughs, the rain just sighs,
As crickets chirp their little lies.
'Who needs to bloom? This is quite fine,
Life's just a jest, with petals divine!'

So here's to the wilted, the bent, and the bruised,
With humor aplenty, none will be mused.
In gardens where giggles make all things last,
We raise our glasses to each wilted past!

Fragile Frames of Time

In frames of time, blooms fade away,
But giggles linger, come what may.
They prance through moments, with tippy toes,
While snapping selfies in bright red bows!

'Hey look at me!' said one little bud,
'Before I'm gone, let's party in mud!'
The daisies gawked, the roses rolled eyes,
'If you're going out, go with surprise!'

With laughter loud and petals flaring,
A dance-off started, all were sharing.
Time may pass, and petals may wilt,
But joy still hangs, from sweet laughter built.

So raise the stakes, and twirl around,
In life's short frame, let humor abound.
When blooms do fade, don't shed a tear,
Just spread your cheer, keep love near!

Serenity in Bloom's Remembrance

In a garden of giggles, blooms sway,
Petals whisper secrets, come what may.
Stumbling bees, tripping on perfume,
Pollination dance, oh what a cartoon!

Sunlight tickles, clouds chuckle bright,
Butterflies flutter, in a dizzy flight.
Roses tease daisies, with colorful flair,
Laughter erupts, floating through the air.

A squirrel swoops in, chasing a dream,
Wearing a hat, oh what a scheme!
Murky puddles turn into a show,
Nature's circus, putting on a glow.

With every bloom, there's a giggling thief,
Stealing smiles, spreading lighthearted grief.
Serenity blooms, in the jolly spree,
Nature's laughter, wild and free.

Silence of the Garden

In the quiet corner, where weeds play chess,
Rabbits steal carrots, oh what a mess!
The daisies are plotting, a prank for the moon,
Whispers of mischief, they'll do it soon.

A fern and a tulip, gossiping low,
Swapping old tales about their woe.
Lost in a breeze, their laughter unfolds,
A secret so juicy, it never gets old.

The garden at night, a raucous delight,
Shimmering shadows, giggling in flight.
When crickets join in, with their chirpy song,
Nature's the party, nothing feels wrong.

In silence, they flourish, this crew of the night,
Frogs wear tuxedos, ready for fright.
What may seem still is a riot inside,
Nature's own comedy, where all can abide.

Dance of the Lost Blossoms

Petals pirouette, lost in a spin,
Swaying to rhythms of laughter within.
Dandelions chuckle, a silly old crew,
Puffing their fluff, as they float on through.

A bumblebee tumbles, what a sight to see,
Buzzing and fumbling, behind a tall tree.
Violets snicker at the blushing rose,
Whispers of charm in their pastel clothes.

The tulips are twirling, beneath sun's embrace,
Launching a challenge, a floral race.
Leaves in the breeze, join the funny parade,
Giggling and jiving, all worries delayed.

Under moonlight's gaze, the garden's alive,
With laughter and joy, we thrive and we jive.
Blossoms lost perhaps, but never the cheer,
Together they twirl, year after year.

Echoes of a Withering Heart

A petal's last dance, with a sigh and a laugh,
Tickled by breezes, its graceful half.
Hummingbirds ponder, with sharp little beaks,
"What's life without laughter?" it joyfully sneaks.

The wilting sunflowers wear frowns so sly,
With droopy old heads, they bid time goodbye.
But every soft whisper, a jest to unfold,
"Dry leaves make good stories, if only retold!"

Echoes of giggles in their softest decay,
Sunbeams and shadows suddenly play.
The fading blooms chuckle at time's cruel jest,
But flowers keep dancing, forever they rest.

As petals drift down, with a flick and a swirl,
A symphony echoing, amidst the world.
For even in endings, joy finds its way,
In every soft whisper, the heart longs to stay.

A Poetic Farewell to Color

In a garden, hues collide,
Each hue whispers, 'No, not my stride!'
Petals chuckle, doing a dance,
While leaves pretend they've lost their chance.

Bees buzz, trying to make a choice,
In a palette with too many a voice.
Who knew green was such a diva?
Declaring war with foliage fever!

Through a riot of shades they parade,
Each bloom flaunts its latest charade.
But as the sun begins to bow,
They sip twilight's drink, and wonder how.

Colorful dramas fade to grey,
Petals giggle, take the day away.
In this garden of bittersweet jest,
Who knew the blooms were comedy's best?

The Final Bow of Nature's Art

When daisies stumble, tripping on dreams,
And sunflowers plot to steal the beams.
With petals askew in their final pose,
They laugh at the bees and their funny prose.

Roses flaunt their majestic flair,
Yet chuckling at thorns while playing fair.
Lilies giggle, with grace they amass,
As violets snicker, 'Wait, do we sass?'

Leaves roll their eyes at this grand charade,
Whispers echo of blooms that just fade.
Nature's art in a perfect jest,
At this farewell, the color's at rest.

Shadows stretch, as night starts to loom,
Yet laughter lingers, filling the room.
In this gallery of wild, they rehearse,
For nature knows, all endings disperse.

Veiled Elegance in Time's Embrace

When petals drape like a silken shawl,
Underneath, whispers of laughter call.
Time gently twirls them, a graceful tease,
As colors blend in a playful breeze.

Faded blooms play peek-a-boo with the sun,
Swaying lightly, they dance just for fun.
Each layer, a joke wrapped tight in a fold,
While memories linger, colorful and bold.

A weeping willow giggles with glee,
As whispers of blooms drift carefree and free.
Nature pens verses in soft, lively strokes,
Where elegance masks the punchlines and jokes.

Yet when twilight raises its curtain high,
With laughter and sighs, the colors comply.
In time's embrace, they bow and depart,
Leaving echoes of joy tucked close to the heart.

Petal's Untold Soliloquy

In a garden of whispers, petals confide,
Sharing secrets, with laughter, they bide.
Each bloom recounts tales of the breeze,
As bees listen in, struggling to tease.

"Oh, the roses," one petal did sigh,
"Always acting as though they could fly!"
While daisies chime in, "We'll take the sun!"
Full of giggles, they bask, just for fun.

Leaves rustle softly, with stories to tell,
Of moments in sunlight, and rain's soft swell.
Petals weave dreams, in swirls of delight,
Lamenting their fate as day turns to night.

Yet through all the mischief and play on display,
These whispers of blooms still color their day.
A soliloquy bursts, where humor rings true,
In the heart of the garden, where laughter renews.

Tapestry of Vanishing Hues

Once vibrant petals wore a frown,
A flower caught in a silly gown.
Dancing in the wind, it swayed,
Who knew flowers could misbehave?

The gardener sighed, what a sight,
This bloom's antics, oh such delight!
With colors fading, it played the fool,
A canvas of chaos, breaking the rule.

Amidst the greens, it stole the show,
With giggles and laughs that seemed to grow.
Chasing butterflies, it tripped on a vine,
A riot of whimsy, truly divine!

Yet as dusk fell, it began to pout,
"Why must my charm begin to drought?"
But even in shadow, you'll forever be
The star of this garden's comedy!

A Melancholic Bloom's Farewell

Beneath the moon, a flower sighed,
It wanted more than petals to hide.
Telling tales to the night-time breeze,
"Why must I wilt with such unease?"

It wore a crown made of wilting leaves,
Daydreaming about what it believes.
A garden party? Oh, what a blast!
But here I am, made of shadows cast.

Twirling in rhythms of poignant prayer,
"Oh please, let me find some springtime air!"
But as it drooped, it couldn't help but grin,
"Maybe I need a few friends in sin!"

With chuckles planted in its grief,
A lilac laugh—what a relief!
"Though my time's up, I had my cheer,
I'll haunt this patch, year after year!"

Disquiet in the Garden's Heart

In the garden, confusion reigned,
The roses joked, "The petunias are drained!"
Each bloom whispered secrets of surprise,
While daisies rolled their silly eyes.

"Who invited that bee?" one tulip exclaimed,
"It buzzes too much, it should be blamed!"
"Let's wave our green arms, be bold, be brave!"
Talk less of honey, more of the rave!

With laughter brightening the leafy space,
Petals fluffed up, a joyous embrace.
"Let's throw a bash!" said the iris in glee,
But the violets just sighed, "Not quite for me!"

As the sun set, they danced till they dropped,
Each bloom with a giggle and whimsy swapped.
In the garden, a ruckus, a heartfelt cheer,
Echoes of laughter, refusing the fear!

The Dimming Glow of Spring

Once in the spring, hues were ablaze,
But now the garden's lost its ways.
"Who turned down the brightness?" a tulip whined,
While the dumb daisies nodded, confused in kind.

"I swear yesterday was a bright sunny day,
But look at us now, all dull and gray!"
A pansy piped up, with a wink and a twist,
"Maybe the sun's gone and made a tryst!"

Giggling glories began a ploy,
"Let's shake off these blues, let's find some joy!
We're blooms, not gloom! Let's have a party!
If we're fading, let's fade out all hearty!"

So they donned their best and spun round and round,
With rustling laughter, joy unbound.
The dimming glow? A giggle in disguise—
For every farewell, a bright new surprise!

Fading Hues in the Afternoon Light

In the garden, I found a wilted friend,
His petals drooped, like a sad weekend.
With lemonade in hand, we'd reminisce,
About the days we danced, in sheer bliss.

Sunlight tickles, then tugs at his tail,
Each color he wears, begins to pale.
We laugh at the weeds that try to intrude,
Yet call him 'King'—his attitude lewd!

Oh, what a journey for this flower bold,
His humor's rich, though he looks quite old.
In the afternoon, fading, he still sways,
Throwing shade on our silly, sad ways.

So here's to the blooms that won't conform,
In laughter and sunshine, they transform.
Together we share these twilight hours,
A fading bloom and his silly powers!

A Sonnet for the Unseen Bloom

A flower in hiding, with potentiel grand,
He never takes photos—oh, isn't that bland?
Behind the tall grasses, he tends to lurk,
His shyness a quirk, like a comical jerk.

His petals are dreamy, yet hard to see,
Like socks in the laundry that flee from me.
We tease him at parties for not showing face,
Yet under the surface, he's all charm and grace.

"Come out!" we all shout, but he won't comply,
The bloom rolls its eyes, like, "Oh, why even try?"
He giggles in silence, a sight rare and true,
A wallflower's laugh is a rare point of view.

To blooms that are hiding, we raise up our cheer,
Your beauty's discovered in absurdity, dear!
So here's to the shadows where blooms like to dwell,
Your laughter's enough—if we can't see you well.

The Quiet Language of Loss

In the silence of gardens, thoughts whirl like bees,
A bloom feels the weight of a soft, gentle breeze.
Whispers of petals that once filled the air,
Now a comedy act with a slight, funny flare.

They dance with the leaves, throwing tantrums of yore,
While a fading flower throws open its door.
With a chuckle, it sighs, shares secrets of gloom,
In a shadowy corner, near an old broom.

The colors that once were start blending with grey,
Yet laughter erupts in a peculiar way.
With a nod and a wink, they craft their own jokes,
In loss, there's a lesson: we're all just old folks.

So here's to the things we thought we should mourn,
They turn into laughter, like a rose with a thorn.
In gardens of quiet, the humor is clear,
It's a funny old life when we shed a sweet tear.

Garden of Solitude and Remembrance

In a garden that's still, where sunflowers plot,
An empty bench waits, oh, why must I rot?
With dandelion wishes that go off the mark,
Each puff tells a story, from light till it's dark.

The tulips are gossiping under their breath,
Saying "Who needs a friend when you've got a pet?"
With squirrels nabbing snacks, and bees buzzing loud,
The untold tales swell—a slightly odd crowd.

An oak tree looks down, with wisdom so grand,
Yet giggles are heard from a weed in the sand.
With roots intertwined, they chat about fate,
Who knew a weed could be such a great mate?

A garden of solitude, laughter runs free,
Remembering blooms, laughing loudly with glee.
In a cycle of life, with each passing hour,
Even loss has a punchline—nature's great power!

www.ingramcontent.com/pod-product-compliance
Lightning Source LLC
Chambersburg PA
CBHW070337120526
44590CB00017B/2914